How to use this book

Follow the advice, in italics, given for you on each page.
Support the children as they read the text that is shaded in cream.
Praise *the children at every step!*

Detailed guidance is provided in the Read Write Inc. Phonics Handbook.

8 reading activities

Children:
- *Practise reading the speed sounds.*
- *Read the green, red and challenge words for the story.*
- *Listen as you read the introduction.*
- *Discuss the vocabulary check with you.*
- *Read the story.*
- *Re-read the story and discuss the 'questions to talk about'.*
- *Re-read the story with fluency and expression.*
- *Practise reading the speed words.*

Speed sounds

Consonants *Say the pure sounds (do not add 'uh').*

f	l	m	n	r	s	v	z	sh	th	ng
ff	(ll)	mm	nn	rr	ss	ve	zz			nk
			kn		ce		s			

b	c	d	g	h	j	p	qu	t	w	x	y	ch
bb	k	dd	gg			pp		tt	wh			tch
	(ck)											

Vowels *Say the vowel sound and then the word, eg 'a', 'at'.*

at	hen	in	on	up	day	see	high	blow
	head					happy		

zoo	look	car	for	fair	whirl	shout	boy

Each box contains one sound but sometimes more than one grapheme. Focus graphemes are **circled**.

Green words

Read in Fred Talk (pure sounds).

s<u>oo</u>n   r<u>oo</u>f   h<u>oo</u>t   <u>th</u>en   sw<u>ay</u>   flo<u>ck</u>   pe<u>ck</u>

Read in syllables.

h<u>oo</u>' ray → h<u>oo</u>ray   ba<u>ll</u>' oon → ba<u>ll</u> <u>oo</u>n   ye<u>ll</u>' <u>ow</u> → ye<u>ll</u> <u>ow</u>

bab' <u>oon</u> → bab<u>oo</u>n   kang' a' r<u>oo</u> → kangar<u>oo</u>

Read the root word first and then with the ending.

cro<u>ss</u> → cro<u>ss</u>es   drift → drifti<u>ng</u>   swim → swi<u>mm</u>i<u>ng</u>

Red words

I'<u>ll</u>   to   <u>th</u>e   he   of   g<u>oe</u>s   sch<u>oo</u>l   so<u>me</u>

Vocabulary check

Discuss the meaning (as used in the story) after the children have read the word.

	definition:
balloon	hot air balloon
baboon	kind of monkey
drifting	being carried along by the wind
swoops	comes down in a sudden, sweeping movement
droops	sags downwards

Punctuation to note in this story:

Sol	Capital letters for names
Hooray Soon Then	Capital letters that start sentences
.	Full stop at the end of each sentence
!	Exclamation mark used to show surprise
...	Wait and see

Sol's balloon

Introduction

Have you ever seen a hot air balloon high up in the sky? You may have even had a flight in one. Sol sets off happily in his balloon and floats high over land and sea, enjoying the view. Suddenly something quite unexpected happens to spoil his flight! Let's find out what happens.

Story written by Cynthia Rider
Illustrated by Tim Archbold

Sol sets off in his yellow balloon.

"Hooray!" he says,

"I'll zoom to the moon!"

Soon Sol is drifting on his way.

He crosses the sand and the ships in the bay.

He drifts past the school

and the roof of a zoo.

He sees a baboon

and a kangaroo.

Then some crows land on the balloon.

Peck, peck, peck!

The balloon goes boom!

A van toot toots as

it sways and swoops.

A bus hoot hoots as

it sinks and droops.

The balloon sinks low but

Sol stays cool …

Splash! He lands in a swimming pool!

Questions to talk about

Re-read the page. Read the question to the children. Tell them whether it is a **FIND IT** question or **PROVE IT** question.

FIND IT	PROVE IT
✓ Turn to the page	✓ Turn to the page
✓ Read the question	✓ Read the question
✓ Find the answer	✓ Find your evidence
	✓ Explain why

Page 8:   FIND IT   Where does Sol say he is going?

Page 9-10: FIND IT   What does the balloon drift past?

Page 10:   FIND IT   What does Sol see in the zoo?

Page 11:   FIND IT   What do the crows do to the balloon?

Page 12:   PROVE IT   What do you think the van driver and the bus driver think of the balloon?